KINDLE UNLIMITED

Users Manual

Is Kindle Unlimited Worth It for You and Your Family?

By Steve Weber

The information in this book is offered with the understanding that it does not contain legal, financial, or other professional advice. Individuals requiring such services should consult a competent professional. The author and publisher make no representations about the suitability of the information contained in this book for any purpose. This material is provided "as is" without warranty of any kind.

Although every effort has been made to ensure the accuracy of the contents of this book, errors and omissions can occur. The publisher assumes no responsibility for any damages arising from the use of this book, or alleged to have resulted in connection with this book.

This book is not completely comprehensive. Some readers may wish to consult additional books for advice. This book is not authorized or endorsed by any company mentioned in the text.

Published by Stephen W. Weber
Weber Books www.WeberBooks.com
ISBN 978-1-936560-24-0

Free Kindle books, all you can eat!

Kindle Buffet is a daily website that features a hand-picked list of great Kindle books being offered free that day, plus dozens more books available at big, temporary discounts. The site includes mysteries, romance, science-fiction, horror, non-fiction and more. Today's bestsellers and yesterday's classics. You may never need to pay for a book again! See for yourself by visiting

www.KindleBuffet.com

kindle buffet

Free books, all you can eat!

Allison (A Kane Novel)

Mystery, Thriller & Suspense
Author: Steve Gannon

Allison Kane, a journalism student at UCLA, takes a summer job as a TV news intern—soon becoming involved in a scandalous murder investigation and the media firestorm that follows—a position that pits her squarely against her iron-fisted police detective father.

Cafenova (Clairmont Series)

Christian Fiction > Romance
Author: S. Jane Scheyder

Leaving her broken heart behind in Seattle, Maddy Jacobs starts a new life on the coast of Maine. Although running a Bed and Breakfast has always been her dream, restoring the sprawling Victorian inn is a massive undertaking. Her contractor, competent, handsome, and built like a Greek god, could be the answer to her prayers. If she can keep her wits about her, she might just survive the summer.

20 Things I've Learned as an Entrepreneur

Small Business & Entrepreneurship
Author: Alicia Morga

20 Things I've Learned as an Entrepreneur is the summary of lessons leading female technology entrepreneur Alicia Morga learned as a first-time entrepreneur in Silicon Valley. If you're an entrepreneur or if you've only dreamed about starting your own business, this quick important read is for you.

Contents

FREE KINDLE BOOKS, ALL YOU CAN EAT! **2**

A NEW WAY TO FEED YOUR NEED TO READ: KINDLE UNLIMITED **5**

IS KINDLE UNLIMITED FOR YOU? **7**

The dearth of selection in KU *9*
KU is more appealing at first *10*
KU books are hard to find *10*
Alternatives to KU *11*
Kindle's best-kept secret: Free loans from your public library *11*
The future of KU *13*

USING KINDLE UNLIMITED STEP-BY-STEP **15**

What kind of hardware do I need to use KU? *15*
What types of books can I find? *15*
Where do I find the KU books? *15*
How do I download a KU book? *15*
How do I return a KU book? *16*
To return a book using Amazon's website: *16*
Can I share my KU subscription with others in my household? *17*
Is KU a good deal for kids? *17*
How do I listen to free KU audiobooks? *17*
How do I know if a KU book includes a free audiobook? *18*
Can I give KU as a gift? *18*
What if the KU gift recipient already has a KU subscription? *19*
What's the procedure for exchanging a KU gift subscription? *19*
What is a KU bundle? *19*
What if the bundle recipient already has a KU subscription? *19*
Are KU bundle recipients automatically upgraded to paid subscriptions after the prepaid period? *19*
Can KU bundles be given as gifts? *19*
Are KU bundle purchases refundable? *20*
How do I cancel KU? *20*
If I cancel, can I get a refund of previous charges? *20*
Is Kindle Unlimited truly unlimited? *20*

THANK YOU! **23**

Make yourself heard *23*

A New Way to Feed Your Need to Read: Kindle Unlimited

Leave it to Amazon to come up with an entirely new value proposition for book lovers—the all-you-can-eat subscription program called Kindle Unlimited.

Kindle Unlimited (from this point forward, abbreviated as **KU**) lets you read as many books as you wish from a library of 1 million titles. About 2,000 of these books also have a free audiobook edition.

Amazon offers a free, 30-day trial membership to KU, enabling you to test-drive the service at no cost for that first month. You can sign up at the Kindle Unlimited page, bit.ly/K-Unlimited

Your subscription will be automatically upgraded to a paid subscription plan unless you cancel before the end of the 30-day trial.

At first blush, Kindle Unlimited is a no-brainer. Just $9.99 a month to read to your heart's content? In what universe is that not a great idea?

Yes, there is a lot to like. With KU, you can spend more time reading and less time shopping. Take me, for instance. Before KU, I used to obsess over buying the "right" book. I'd spend lots of time researching book reviews and scouting competing books before I ever broke down and bought one. In some cases, I probably spent more time shopping for the book than I actually spent reading it.

Why did I go through this rigmarole? My pet peeve was getting stuck with a book I didn't like. (All of that wasted time and money—the humanity!) So I invested untold hours trying to avoid the duds. Well, KU can eliminate such chores. As soon as you get a whiff of a potential read, you download it and plow right in. If it's not up to snuff, you just move on to the next one. No angst, no wasted money.

Books aren't the only thing picky folks like me agonize over. I used to spend countless hours prowling the aisles at Blockbuster stores, doing much the same thing—searching for a decent movie amid the stinkers. I'd waste gobs of time researching a potential movie rental, because I just couldn't bear getting home and discovering I'd rented a bomb. Still, it happened way too often.

Enter Netflix. Now you don't even need to leave your easy chair. You just skim the list of videos, pick one, and dive in. Sure, most of the Netflix lineup is garbage. But if you accidentally start watching a dud, it's not the end of the world. You just move on to the next one. Kind of like KU.

Unfortunately, KU and Netflix are more alike than you might expect. Most KU books are junk, too. KU doesn't include all of Amazon's Kindle catalog, not by a long shot. In fact, most of KU's lineup is self-published fiction from authors you've never heard of—including many, many books that should never see the light of day. But deep within, there are nuggets of gold.

So yes, KU can do you two big favors: first, cutting the time you spend finding new reading material, and secondly, cutting the price you pay for it. It just depends on how voracious a reader you are, and how picky you are.

By reading this book, you'll probably learn whether KU will work for you. We'll examine the good, the bad, and the ugly. And, just as importantly, I'll let you know about several alternatives you might like even better than KU, including one that won't cost you a dime!

So let's dive right to it, shall we?

Is Kindle Unlimited for You?

KU appeals most strongly to avid readers. No surprise there. But is it right for you?

At first glance, it would seem that KU is easily worth the money—it costs just $9.99 a month. Even if you're a slow reader (like me), you can probably polish off two or three books a month without breaking a sweat. Perhaps with a "free" supply of reading material, you'll also step up your game, and read even more books.

Oh, if it were only that simple.

KU's stable includes lots of cheapies

Two major problems with KU: First, it's harder than you'd expect to find KU-eligible books—there's no "store" or recommendation system dedicated to KU books. And secondly, KU's selection is limited—it includes very few books by famous authors.

But let's say you're patient enough to unearth lots of KU books—how many KU books must you read to get your money's worth? Let's run some numbers. First, consider the annual cost of KU, about $120 annually. And let's say the average cost of a Kindle book is $6. You'll need to read 20 books during the year to recoup your investment.

The average American reads five books per year according to recent poll. But let's assume you're a voracious reader, and knocking out 20 books a year is easy. The question is, can you find enough KU books that interest you?

Here's a quick experiment: Run through the list of books you've purchased over the past year. To see a list of your Amazon Kindle purchases, visit bit.ly/KindleOrders . Here are the books you've spent your hard-earned dollars on.

Now, determine how many of those books you bought are KU-eligible. Probably not too many. Personally, I bought 27 Kindle books during 2014, and just four of those are available through Kindle Unlimited.

Here's another way to evaluate KU's value. Instead of looking at your previous purchases, consider your Amazon wishlist (if you have one) or your Goodreads "want to read" list. How many of those books are in KU? Not many, right?

Why the dearth of selection in KU? Quite simply, leading authors aren't in the program because it doesn't pay them enough. Danielle Steel? No. Nora Roberts? Nope. Robert Ludlum? Nada. James Patterson, John Grisham, Dan Brown, Ken Follett, Stephenie Meyer, Mary Higgins Clark, Patricia Cornwell, Tom Clancy, Janet Evanovich or Dr. Seuss? Sorry, Charlie.

Oh, and this leads to another complication. Most of the no-name books included in KU are already priced low—$2.99 and under. So you'll have to read at least 40 books a year to make KU pay off, not the 20 books we assumed earlier.

Now certainly, one thing we've overlooked in this exercise: the availability of KU would likely increase your consumption of books. You just might discover five or more "favorite" authors over the course of the next year during your use of KU. You might feel the freedom to sample a genre that you've never explored before. One or more of these new books might, quite literally, change your life. That, after all, is the power of reading.

Above: Here's a portion of Amazon's product page for a book. If the book is KU-eligible, it will have the two features circled above: the KU logo at the left, and the "Read for Free" button at the right.

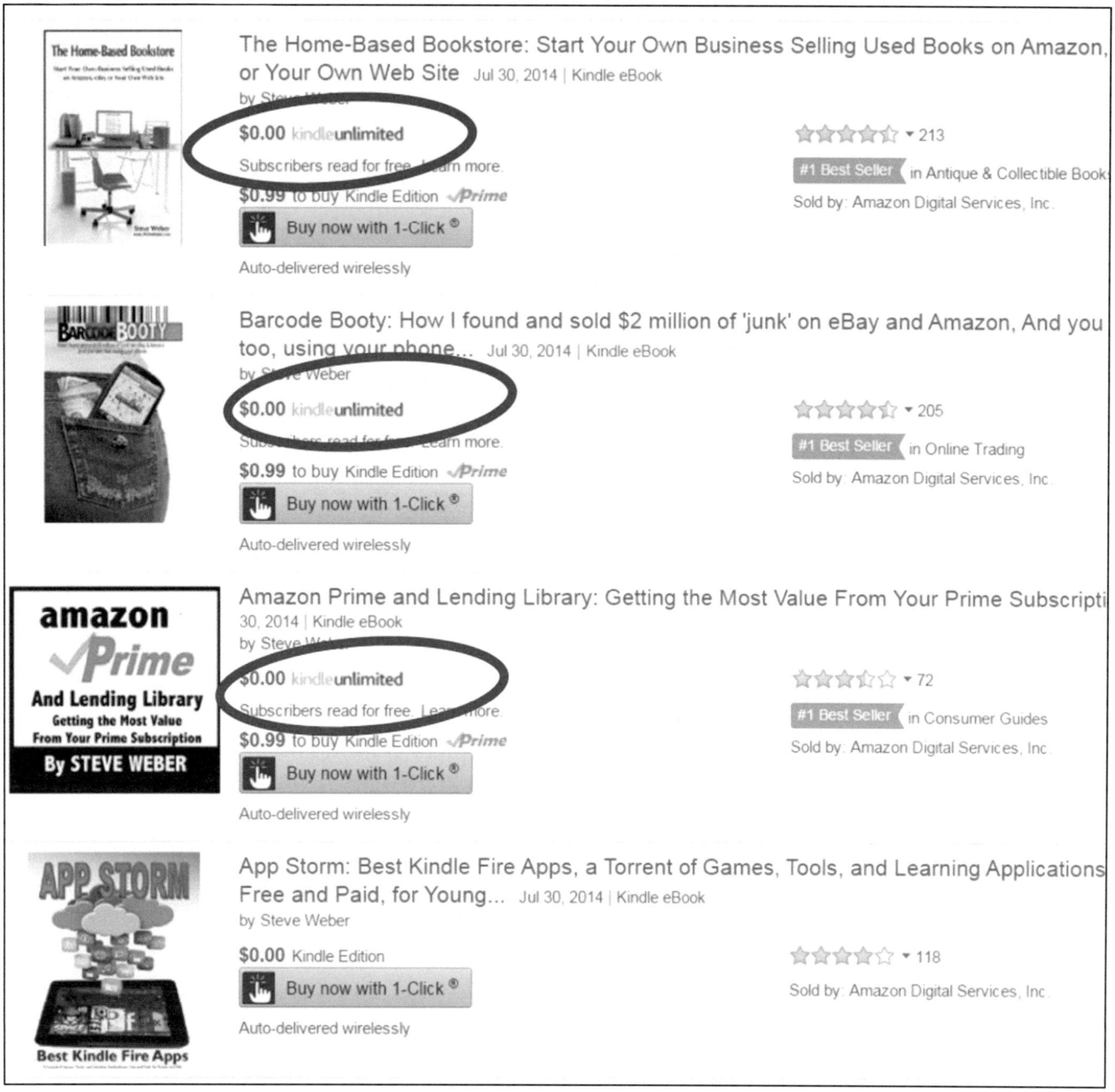

Above: Here's another way to identify KU-eligible books. The image above shows Amazon's search results for the author name "Steve Weber." KU books are identified by the logo under the author name.

The dearth of selection in KU

Why doesn't KU include the popular books most people want to read? It's simple: KU pays authors and publishers a pittance compared to what they're used to. KU pays about $1.35 per book to authors instead of the $2 to $8 per book these folks are used to. As a result, the "big five" publishing houses—HarperCollins, Hachette, Macmillan, Penguin Random House and

Simon & Shuster—aren't in KU. The KU catalog includes about 1 million titles, compared to the 3.5 million Kindle books available otherwise.

Now, you might be muttering to yourself, "KU would be doing just fine if it weren't for those greedy authors and publishers." Perhaps. But this won't change overnight. As a result, KU is saddled with lots of books from relatively unknown authors who often don't have the resources to pay for professional editors, proofreaders, and audiobook narrators.

KU is more appealing at first

During your first month, the free trial, you might be looking at KU through rose-colored glasses. The program seems awesome in the beginning, partly because of some special deals Amazon has arranged with a few famous authors. Amazon bought the rights to add Harry Potter, Lord of the Rings, and Hunger Games to KU, and these books are displayed prominently. After that, the hits are few and far between. Not a single major publisher in the United States has signed onto KU. (If Amazon were able to attract one or two of the biggies, the value of KU would increase considerably.)

KU books are hard to find

Not only are there few books available through KU, Amazon hasn't made KU-eligible books easy to find. There's a KU logo that appears on the book's webpage, but the logo doesn't appear on most category pages or bestseller rankings—making KU books sometimes as hard to find as a needle in a haystack.

One of the greatest things about Amazon is its book recommendation system. The website suggests books based on your previous purchases and ratings—visit the address: bit.ly/KindleRecommendations. But which one of these books are available through KU? There's no way to know unless you click through to each one, a tedious process.

You can also browse part of the KU catalog by using a Kindle device. Click on the shopping-cart logo, then look under the **Featured** heading for **Kindle Unlimited**. You'll see a list of books, which you can sort by popularity, genre, customer rating, or release date. For KU-eligible books, you'll find the Kindle Unlimited logo alongside the book: kindleunlimited. Unfortunately, if you search for a specific title or author, your search results will include non-KU books.

Alternatives to KU

Although Amazon's Kindle system undoubtedly has the broadest selection of eBooks, some competing subscription programs offer more of the books from major publishers.

Entitle (www.entitlebooks.com) has the best selection of bestsellers, including new releases from HarperCollins and Simon & Shuster. You can access up to two books at a time for $9.99 a month, three books at a time for $14.99 per month, or 24 for $99 a year. Also, Entitle works with Barnes & Noble Nook eReaders, while other services mentioned here require an Android or Apple device.

Oyster (www.oysterbooks.com) has a fantastic selection of older books, but not many current bestsellers. The company charges $9.95 a month for unlimited access to its catalog using an app. Oyster claims about 500,000 titles. No titles from major publishers.

Scribd (www.scribd.com) provides access to 400,000 documents for $8.99 a month. No titles from major publishers.

Kindle's best-kept secret: Free loans from your public library

The advent of eBooks was supposed to put the old-fashioned public library out of business, according to many pundits. But somebody forgot to tell the libraries this, and meanwhile they've been building collections for their customers who enjoy Kindle books and other digital content.

OverDrive (www.overdrive.com) an eBook service affiliated with thousands of local public libraries, enabling them to loan Kindle books and audiobooks. That's right, at most libraries nowadays you can borrow Kindle books at no charge, without even leaving the house. The best part: the collection of Kindle books available at most libraries includes bestsellers and classics from your favorite authors—precisely those books missing from KU.

Signing up for OverDrive is easy: First, download the app or go to their website and enter your library branch and card number. It's a service you're subsidizing with your tax dollars, so there's no reason not to try it.

Here's a variation of the experiment we discussed earlier: Go through a list of the books you've purchased over the past year. How many of them are available as a free Kindle loan from your library? More than you might expect.

The selection of Kindle books varies from library to library. Libraries in high-population areas tend to have a better selection, but many rural libraries have a nice collection too. And you're not necessarily limited to local library branches—in most states you can obtain a library card outside your immediate area at no extra charge. Also, several urban libraries will issue cards to out-of-state residents, although sometimes an annual fee is charged. For example, the Brooklyn Public Library, in New York, has an excellent selection of Kindle books and issues cards through the mail to any U.S. resident who pays an annual $50 fee. For a list of such libraries, consult this page: bit.ly/ebookLoans .

If you've tried checking out eBooks from the library in the past and have been disappointed, you should try again. Libraries have beefed up their digital selection tremendously in the past few years. Who knows, after you exhaust the available Kindle books at your local library, you might not have any time left to peruse KU.

I recently checked to see which of the top 10 books on the *New York Times* bestseller list were available through KU. Not a single one. But all 10 of those bestsellers were available as a Kindle loan through my local library. And of those 10 books, nine were also available as an audiobook download from my library. Buying those audiobooks from Amazon would have cost $218.55, whether I had a KU subscription or not.

But perhaps you don't read bestsellers; perhaps you prefer a steady diet of something more specific—like military science-fiction pulp novels. Maybe you're into kinky erotica. In that case you'll likely find a steady diet of such fare on KU alone.

In some ways your library's OverDrive service and KU are complementary. OverDrive tends to provide access to popular, mainstream books that librarians know will be in demand with a high percentage of their patrons. Meanwhile, KU includes books that simply aren't available to libraries—including quirky, innovative books from up-and-coming authors.

Although you don't need to physically visit the library to borrow Kindle books via OverDrive, you might have to wait in a virtual line for popular books. Libraries have a limited number of licenses for each eBook, so if all the available copies are checked out, you'll need to place a "hold" on the book, just as you would with a hardcover book.

Kindle Owners' Lending Library is Amazon's version of a public library. If you're not a voracious reader, the Kindle Owners' Lending Library, also called KOLL, might satisfy your appetite. KOLL allows you to borrow one Kindle book per month at no charge, and the selection is very similar to KU's.

KOLL is included as part of Amazon Prime, a membership program that includes several benefits, including free streaming music, online movies and TV shows, and discounted shipping. KOLL isn't worth the annual $99 Prime fee by itself, but it's a nice extra.

Another feature of KOLL is **Kindle First**, which lets you download one newly published Kindle book per month before the title is publicly available. Subscribers choose from among four titles announced at the beginning of each month. The books are usually popular fiction from famous authors.

To access KOLL from your Kindle device, open the Kindle store. Under **All Categories**, select **Kindle Owners' Lending Library**.

Another detail about KOLL: you need a Kindle device to use it, unlike KU, which works with any device using a free Kindle reading app. Also, a Prime subscription is required to access KOLL, but Prime isn't a prerequisite for KU.

And don't forget, you can download the first section of any Kindle book for free by clicking the **Send Sample** button at Amazon. What better way to decide if you want to purchase the book and continue reading. It's also a good way to "save" a list of books you're considering.

The future of KU

Will Amazon be able to improve the selection of books available through KU? It's impossible to know. Some authors have been disappointed with the revenue from KU and have withdrawn their titles. Many of these authors are accustomed to getting $3 to $6 in royalties each time an Amazon customer downloads one of their books, while KU pays only about $1.35 per download.

On the other hand, several authors have been quite successful with KU by serializing their work. Instead of publishing a 100,000-word novel, for example, these authors break their story into several smaller chunks, with each part being a separate Kindle download. The royalty from these shorter volumes is the same as a longer book. So authors publishing serials can earn lots more money—as long as they hook readers on the series. Meanwhile, the KU subscribers happily download each part since it costs them nothing extra.

Fiction serialization began in the Victorian era, when many novels first appeared as monthly or weekly installments in newspapers or magazines. The success of Charles Dickens' *The Pickwick Papers*, which first appeared in the 1830s, established the viability of serialized literature. Back then, the innovation of movable type slashed the cost of publishing, and today eBooks have done the same thing by eliminating printing and distribution costs.

Some nonfiction authors have also exploited KU by producing shorter works, sometimes even selling each chapter as a Kindle "book." Some Kindle books are no longer than an average magazine article, but the KU subscriber doesn't feel shortchanged because each book costs them nothing extra.

Using Kindle Unlimited Step-by-Step

Now for the fine print. To use KU, you must have an Amazon account with a current, valid credit card with 1-Click payments enabled. To enable 1-Click, visit bit.ly/AmazonOneClick . One exception to the 1-Click requirement is if you have a prepaid KU subscription (a gift or bundle).

What kind of hardware do I need to use KU?

You can use any Kindle device or virtually any smartphone or tablet using Amazon's free Kindle application. You can also view Kindle books on a desktop computer or laptop using your Web browser.

What types of books can I find?

Genre fiction is the lion's share of KU. If you're looking for mystery, romance, thrillers, science fiction, historical fiction, erotica, classics, or young-adult stuff, you're in business. If you're looking for something more specific, you'll also find fantasy, steampunk, cyberpunk, horror, chick lit, true crime, literary—you'll find all of it.

It's obvious that erotica is among the most popular type of KU book. Is that because all the best erotica is available only in KU, or is it because most people are too embarrassed to buy such a book in person? I have no idea, you be the judge.

Where do I find the KU books?

1. On your device or reading app, open the Kindle Store. On e-Ink Kindles with black-and-white screens, the Kindle Store is represented by a shopping cart icon. Select **All Categories**, then select **Kindle Unlimited**.

2. If you're using a Kindle Fire tablet, select **Kindle Unlimited.** On a free Kindle reading app on your smartphone or tablet, go to **Store** and then **Kindle Unlimited**.

3. Select a book, then select **Read for Free**. Eligible books have a Kindle Unlimited logo.

You can also browse KU books with a web browser by visiting bit.ly/KUbooks .

How do I download a KU book?

1. From your Kindle device or reading app, open the **Kindle Store**.

2. Access the KU catalog using this method:

- For Kindle eReaders such as the Paperwhite or Voyage, select **All Categories**, then select **Kindle Unlimited**.
- Using a Kindle Fire tablet, Select **Kindle Unlimited**.
- Using a Kindle reading app on your phone or tablet: Select **Kindle Unlimited**.

3. Select a book, then choose **Read for Free**. (The KU logo will alert you to eligible books.)

You can also search for KU books on Amazon's website. Visit the KU browse page, bit.ly/KUbooks . The KU logo will alert you to eligible books: kindleunlimited.

On the product webpage for the book, select **Read for Free**, located below the familiar **Buy** button.

How do I return a KU book?

KU books don't have due dates, but you're limited to 10 books at a time. You can return a book directly from your Kindle or on Amazon's website.

Using your Kindle device or reading app:

1. Visit the Kindle Store.
2. Navigate to the KU landing page using this method:

- Using a Kindle eReader such as the Paperwhite or Voyage, select **All Categories**, then select **Kindle Unlimited**.
- Using a Kindle Fire tablet: Select **Kindle Unlimited**.
- Using a Kindle reading app on your smartphone or tablet, select **Kindle Unlimited**.

To return a book using Amazon's website:

1. Navigate to: bit.ly/ManageContentDevices .
2. From the **Your Content** area, use the drop-down menu to select among **Kindle Unlimited**, and then **Books**.
3. Next to the book you want to return, select **Actions**, then **Return this book**.

Can I share my KU subscription with others in my household?

Yes. You can store up to 10 KU books simultaneously on as many as six devices.

The "easy" way to share Kindle books with other family members is to register multiple Kindle devices with the same Amazon email address. For example, in my household, each Kindle device—mine, my wife's, our young daughter's—is registered to my Amazon email address. My account is used for all Kindle purchases, so each book we buy is automatically shared among all the Kindles in our household. It's convenient, but the adults in the household must take care not to purchase content that is inappropriate for youngsters.

Another way to share Kindle books is to use the **Family Library** function. Family Library adds more control—books may still be shared, but certain content may remain private. For example, you can link two accounts to a single device, which can enable a spouse and partner to share books. Meanwhile, those two folks can jointly supervise and control the accounts of as many as four children.

The only slight drawback with Family Library is that it takes some time to set up. For more details, visit bit.ly/FamilyLibrary .

Is KU a good deal for kids?

It depends. On the bright side, kids in your household can share your KU subscription. So if your children are accustomed to reading Kindle books, they'll certainly find some fodder on KU. Unfortunately, KU's selection of kids' books is just as lacking as its selection for adults. Sure, there are some exceptions, like *Life of Pi* and *Diary of a Wimpy Kid*, but most bestselling children's authors haven't ventured into KU.

If your kids consume lots of digital content, you might also investigate **Freetime Unlimited**, which provides access to 8,000 kid-friendly books, movies, TV shows, educational apps and games. The cost is $4.99 per month or $2.99 a month for Prime subscribers.

How do I listen to free KU audiobooks?

If you've downloaded a KU title that includes a free companion audiobook, you'll automatically have access to the audio. You can listen on most Kindle devices, reading apps, and using the Audible.com app. Depending on the device you're using, you may be able to seamlessly switch between the text and audio. Amazon's Whispersync for Voice keeps track of your progress , and automatically begins the book at the precise point you've left off using either the text or audio.

KU includes about 2,000 free audiobooks. But most of the audiobooks at Amazon cost extra because they're from Audible.com, which is owned by Amazon. Audible boasts 180,000 titles, including new releases and bestsellers.

New KU members get a free three-month trial to Audible.com. With this free trial, you get one free Audible audiobook for each of those three months. After the trial, Audible.com membership costs $14.95 a month, which lets you listen to one audiobook per month, and buy additional audiobooks at a 30-percent discount off the retail price.

How do I know if a KU book includes a free audiobook?

On the book's product page, beside the Kindle Unlimited icon, you'll see the words **with narration**.

Also, you can browse all the KU books available with free audio at bit.ly/NarratedBooks .

To view KU books with free and paid audio versions, visit the KU browse page, bit.ly/KUbooks .

Under **Refine by**, select **Whispersync for Voice**.

By the way, if you have a Kindle Fire tablet, you can access the **text-to-speech** function, another way to listen to many KU books. The robotic voice isn't anything like a professional narrator, but it's nice to have sometimes—if you really want to listen to a particular book while driving, for example. To find out whether a Kindle book includes text-to-speech, visit the **Product Details** area of the book's Amazon webpage. Enrolled books will have the notation **Text-to-speech: Enabled**. In addition to Kindle Fire tablets, the text-to-speech feature also works on some older Kindle devices with headphone jacks.

Can I give KU as a gift?

Yes, you can purchase a KU gift subscription good for six, 12 or 24 months. Follow these steps:

1. Visit www.amazon.com/kindleunlimitedgift .
2. Select Give the gift of Kindle Unlimited.

3. Continue to checkout and enter your account and payment data.

4. Enter the e-mail address of the gift recipient, a personal message, and request a delivery date anytime within the next year. The recipient must be a U.S. resident. They must have an Amazon account, but not necessarily an account registered with the gift email address.

What if the KU gift recipient already has a KU subscription?

When the gift subscription is redeemed, the recipient's existing paid subscription will be paused for the duration of the gift. If the recipient wishes, they can exchange the value of the gift subscription for an Amazon gift card.

What's the procedure for exchanging a KU gift subscription?

1. Open the gift email from Amazon and click Redeem your Kindle Unlimited Gift membership.

2. In the new window, sign into your Amazon account.

3. Beneath the **Redeem** button, click the link to **Exchange for an Amazon gift card**.

What is a KU bundle?

KU subscriptions are available at discounted prices when a customer purchases certain Kindle devices. For example, one offer enables customers to pre-pay for six months of KU at a discount. The subscription begins when the customer clicks the activation link in an email Amazon sends.

What if the bundle recipient already has a KU subscription?

Their KU billing is paused until the expiration of the pre-paid period.

Are KU bundle recipients automatically upgraded to paid subscriptions after the prepaid period?

No. If you've never had a monthly subscription, you're prompted to upgrade at the end of the prepaid period, but aren't automatically enrolled.

Can KU bundles be given as gifts?

Yes. You can purchase one for yourself, designate a gift recipient by entering their email during the purchase, or split the bundle between two recipients. Bundle recipients can exchange the value of the bundle for an Amazon gift card. For more details, consult the web page bit.ly/KUgift .

Are KU bundle purchases refundable?

Yes, you can request an Amazon gift card in lieu of redeeming the KU gift.

How do I cancel KU?

Visit the **Your Account** section of Amazon's website, www.amazon.com/youraccount and follow this procedure:

1. Click on **Manage Your Content and Devices** near the bottom of the page.
2. Select the **Settings** tab and scroll down to **Kindle Unlimited Settings**.
3. Select Cancel Kindle Unlimited.

Amazon will debit your account unless you notify the company before then that you want to cancel. Otherwise, your membership automatically renews without notice to you. Amazon will collect the money on membership fees and any applicable taxes using any of the credit cards they have on file for you. If your bank declines the transactions, your membership will be canceled unless you register a new card with Amazon. If you pay your membership fee late with a new card, your membership period is based on the original renewal date, not the date of the transaction against your new card.

When you cancel a KU subscription, your benefits continue until the next billing due date. After the billing date passes, the KU titles you've downloaded will automatically be removed from your Kindle devices and applications. However, your notes, highlights and bookmarks are preserved, and you can use them if you access one of the books in the future.

If I cancel, can I get a refund of previous charges?

No. You can cancel at any time, but cancellation doesn't entitle you to a refund of any membership fees already paid.

Is Kindle Unlimited truly unlimited?

Not really. You're allowed access to only 10 titles at a time. (Most public libraries have a similar limit on access to eBooks and physical books.) Further, if Amazon suspects "fraud," such as the transferring of membership benefits with other readers, the company reserves the right to restrict the number of titles you can access at any one time. If you download more than 1,000 books per month, Amazon will suspect fraud.

Amazon reserves the right to cancel your membership at its discretion without notice. In that case, you'd receive a pro-rated refund based on the days remaining on your membership. But Amazon won't refund you anything if the company determines you've violated the terms of the membership or have committed "fraud or misuse" of the program.

Thank You!

Thanks for taking the time to read this book. I hope it has helped you make an informed choice about KU and its alternatives.

Make yourself heard

Perhaps you've got a suggestion for how Amazon can improve KU. Send an email to kindle-feedback@amazon.com, and your message will be carefully evaluated. And while you're at it, if you have a suggestion on how I might improve future editions of this book, please drop me a line at steve@weberbooks.com .

Book Lovers, Rejoice: Free Books!

Kindle Buffet is a daily website that features a hand-picked list of great Kindle books being offered free that day. Includes mysteries, romance, science-fiction, horror, non-fiction and more. Today's bestsellers and yesterday's classics. You may never need to pay for a book again! See for yourself by visiting www.KindleBuffet.com

kindle buffet

Free books, all you can eat!

Allison (A Kane Novel)

Mystery, Thriller & Suspense
Author: Steve Gannon

Allison Kane, a journalism student at UCLA, takes a summer job as a TV news intern—soon becoming involved in a scandalous murder investigation and the media firestorm that follows—a position that pits her squarely against her iron-fisted police detective father.

Cafenova (Clairmont Series)

Christian Fiction > Romance
Author: S. Jane Scheyder

Leaving her broken heart behind in Seattle, Maddy Jacobs starts a new life on the coast of Maine. Although running a Bed and Breakfast has always been her dream, restoring the sprawling Victorian inn is a massive undertaking. Her contractor, competent, handsome, and built like a Greek god, could be the answer to her prayers. If she can keep her wits about her, she might just survive the summer.

20 Things I've Learned as an Entrepreneur

Small Business & Entrepreneurship
Author: Alicia Morga

20 Things I've Learned as an Entrepreneur is the summary of lessons leading female technology entrepreneur Alicia Morga learned as a first-time entrepreneur in Silicon Valley. If you're an entrepreneur or if you've only dreamed about starting your own business, this quick important read is for you.